Introduction

Welcome to **Here Come the Vikings!**, a unit in the topic-based series **Eureka!**. The three programmes in the unit offer an opportunity to explore the Viking world and to dispel some of the myths that surround it. Programme 1 focuses on where the Vikings came from and where they went. Programme 2 looks at what Viking life was like for people living in Britain. Programme 3 investigates the evidence that helps us to form a picture of the Viking Age.

This Teachers' Guide offers background information about the period and suggestions for further reading. The notes for each programme give a synopsis of the programme, learning outcomes and suggestions for work before, during and after the programme. Two photocopiable factfiles and two activity sheets are provided for each programme. The factfiles may be used for background information or could become the focus of a particular activity.

We hope that you enjoy watching Here Come the Vikings! and find the unit a helpful resource in the classroom.

Channel 4 Schools is keen to ensure that programmes transmitted are of a high quality and that support materials are well focused. We therefore welcome comments and suggestions about the programmes and the accompanying support materials. These can be sent to me at the address below.

Anne Fleck
Education Officer
Channel 4 Schools
PO Box 100
Warwick
CV34 6TZ

contents

🦻 **Subtitles**
This Channel 4 Schools series is subtitled on page 888 of Teletext for the deaf and hearing-impaired.

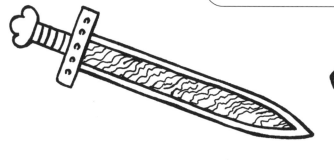

About the series

The three programmes in this series look at the impact of Viking settlements on the history of the British Isles. This is set in the context of Viking migrations; therefore the changes seen in Britain are linked to the developments within the wider Viking world and also linked with areas outside the Viking world but with which the Vikings came into contact.

The programmes explore aspects of Viking life and society through several stages of an archaeological dig which is in progress in the Shetland Islands. This approach enables us to demonstrate the importance of archaeological evidence in response to the historical question 'How do we know?'.

Learning objectives

● To gain a sense of the extent of the Viking world (both where they settled and the world they knew through trade and travel).

● To gain a sense of continuity and of the chronological extent of the Viking influence in Europe.

● To develop an understanding of some of the characteristic features of Viking society.

● To learn about some of the changes and developments which took place during the Viking period.

● To consider and interrogate some of the ways in which the Vikings have been represented in history.

● To become aware of the range of sources, both primary and secondary, available for any study of the Vikings. In particular, to understand the importance of archaeological evidence, and understand some of the ways in which it can be used and interpreted.

● To begin to formulate historical questions.

The Vikings and the curriculum

The Vikings can either be taught as a single topic or as part of a broader study of migration and the development of an ethnically and culturally diverse society in Britain. In some cases, this will include the migration to Britain of the Romans and Anglo-Saxons.

As a result of little or no contemporary documentary evidence, the Viking era, along with the Anglo-Saxon era, is somewhat shrouded in mystery and so has been characterised as the 'Dark Ages' of British history. However, there are alternative sources of evidence (particularly archaeological) and it is these that children can investigate and thus develop the concept of historical interpretation.

The level at which these ideas are explored will vary with the age, experience and aptitude of the children, but for all of them the questions 'What do we know?' and 'How do we know?' will be central.

Depending on where your school is located and on what resources are available locally, you might be able to exploit your local area to give the Viking period some substance. However, if the opportunities are limited (though you'd be amazed at where the Vikings got to!), then sites such as Jorvik (York) produce a lot of resource materials which will enable you to study a settlement. Similarly, the British Museum in London produces useful information and resource materials which can be used in the classroom.

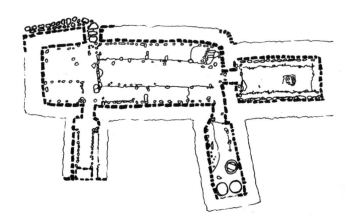

The Vikings in the curriculum

England

Key Stage 2 (originally statutory but now relaxed to allow greater flexibility)

Study Unit 1: Romans, Anglo-Saxons and Vikings in Britain
1:1c Viking raids and settlements
1:2c Viking raids and settlement and their impact on the British Isles
everyday life; the legacy of Viking settlement

Study Unit 5: Local history

Wales

Key Stage 2

Study Unit 1: Life in Early Wales and Britain
1:3 Vikings
Viking invasions and settlements
Life in Wales and Britain at the time of the Vikings

Study Unit 4: A study of an historical issue or topic in a local context

Study Unit 5: A study of an historical theme
5:2 a) Houses and households
b) Writing and reading
c) Food and farming

Scotland

Primary 4-6

Environmental Studies 5-14 Social Subjects: Understanding people in the past:
– The Middle Ages (400-1450) studying people, events and societies of significance in the past;
– developing an understanding of change and continuity, cause and effect;
– developing an understanding of time and historical sequence;
– developing an understanding of the nature of historical evidence;
– considering the meaning of heritage.

Northern Ireland

Key Stage 2

Study Unit: The Vikings – focusing on the nature of Viking society in Scandinavia and the impact of Viking raiders and settlers on Ireland and elsewhere.

a) Viking way of life at home
b) Viking expansion and settlement abroad
c) Vikings-related (or not) topic

Background information

The name

The Scandinavians we call the 'Vikings' did not use that name for themselves. They generally identified themselves with the particular districts they came from. Even the derivation of the word is uncertain, though it is possibly linked with seafaring. 'Vik' or 'Wick' (meaning 'bay') is still found in many British, as well as Scandinavian, place names (Sandvik: sandy bay; Lerwick: clay bay).

In Old Norse (the language of ancient Scandinavians), a Viking was a raider and going 'a-viking' meant sailing out pursuing plunder and prestige. These people lived in a brutal age and were skilled at making violence serve their ends. However, characters like Egil Skalagrimsson could combine murderous lifestyles with refined cultural sensibilities. The majority of Vikings were not full-time raiders. Many were peaceful farmers, fishers, craftworkers or traders. Others joined a few raids to get enough wealth to develop other enterprises or acquire land.

Raids

It was through raiding that the Vikings first appeared in written records. These started with the raid in AD793 on the island monastery of Lindisfarne (near today's English-Scottish border). Over the next few decades, monks chronicled attacks in England, Ireland, France, Spain, Portugal and Italy. Then, between 800 and 1100, the Vikings travelled the Northern Hemisphere more extensively than anyone had ever done before. This period, when they were a major influence on the course of European history, is widely regarded as the core of the Viking Age.

At the start, their raids were small and uncoordinated. By the end, thousands had left their homelands, settling over vast distances, with lasting implications for international culture, commerce and politics.

Swedish Vikings

The Swedes looked primarily eastwards, pursuing trade. From colonies across the Baltic, they used river routes to go to the Caspian Sea and Constantinople (now Istanbul). They even traded in Baghdad. Russia is named after 'The Rus', the name Slavs gave to Rurik's Swedish settlers.

Norwegian Vikings

The land-hungry Norwegians mostly looked westward, settling in Scotland, Ireland, Iceland and even Greenland. Though the North Atlantic climate is harsh, they had learned to cope with it in their homeland, and preferred to settle there rather than around the Mediterranean, with its very different environmental problems.

Danish Vikings

The Danes were interested in Ireland, Wales and especially the east of England. Other parts of England and France saw both Norwegian and Danish activity.

The resettlements

Long before the 8th century raids, the Scandinavians had traded widely, and there may have been some peaceful settlements in the British Isles. So why did their dramatic emigration and resettlement occur? There seems to be no single answer. Together, the homelands of the Vikings (Norway, Sweden and Denmark) stretch nearly 2000km north-south.

Geography, however, sets severe constraints on agriculture. Good land was scarce, even for the two million people (approximately) in Scandinavia at the start of the Viking Age. Northern Norway is far inside the Arctic Circle and major mountains fill both Norway and north-western Sweden. Central and southern Sweden has arable potential, but in Norway this is restricted to occasional patches along the craggy fjord coast. Denmark, though mountain-free, has extensive infertile sandy heaths as well as some good land.

Paradoxically, it was not a deteriorating, but an improving, climate which highlighted these geographical limitations. With good harvests, people lived longer and more children survived, so population pressure increased rapidly. Sociological factors also contributed; primogeniture laws forced out younger sons and banishment overseas was a punishment for feuding. Then, in the 9th century, when King Harald Finehair dominated Norway with his large army, sagas tell of independent-minded families emigrating to Orkney and Iceland.

Religion

The conversion of Vikings to Christianity gained momentum from the reign of Harald Bluetooth in the mid-10th century. The burning or burial of a chieftain in a ship is a popular image of 'pagan Viking religion' but archaeological and literary evidence suggest that there was a wide variety of rituals. Odin and Thor were just part of a complex pantheon, with regional variations, much like the religions of the ancient Greeks and Romans, and of many modern peoples, such as the Hindus.

The old religion will never be fully understood, because the written evidence only comes from the Christians of later centuries. Interestingly, we know less archaeologically about the lifestyles and trade patterns of later Vikings than earlier ones, because, with the coming of Christian burial, we lose the remarkable evidence of pagan grave goods.

The end of the Viking Age

The 11th century is often seen as the end of the Viking Age, but this is an oversimplification. It faded away, at different times in different places. For example, in Ireland Viking Dublin maintained some independence until the late 12th-century English conquest. Only in 1266 were the Hebrides and Isle of Man ceded by Norway to Scotland. Shetland and Orkney remained integral parts of Scandinavia until 1468/9, while the last Norse settlements in Greenland probably survived even longer.

In England, Harald Hardrada's attempt to reassert Scandinavian control in 1066 failed. However, the Normans, whose victory over the English later that year changed the course of British history, were actually of Viking ancestry: 'North-men' who had settled in France where Normandy was named after them.

There is, nevertheless, much to justify the view that the late 11th century saw the ending of several important aspects of the Viking Age. By then, settlers had taken up most of the better land in the North Atlantic islands. In areas with stronger indigenous cultures, from Russia to Ireland, generations of integration had led those of Scandinavian ancestry to identify with the areas they had settled, with little enthusiasm for further expansionist adventures. The era of easy pickings for small raiding parties was over, and even large Viking armies had been successfully countered.

Major developments to the south of Europe were also impinging upon Scandinavia, so that from an area which initiated changes it became one which reflected them. Denmark, set at the edge of the European plain, was especially open to such influences. By the 11th century, it was already developing as a unified Christian state ruled by a single monarch, with land held by his feudal lords instead of by ordinary families. Unlike its old Viking trading emporium at Hedeby, its new towns at Arhus and Roskilde were royally-controlled political and administrative centres.

Thus, by the end of the 11th century, the Vikings – the most powerful force in north-west Europe in the 9th and 10th centuries – were becoming the northerly periphery of feudal Christendom.

The Viking legacy

Despite their reputation as mere raiders, the Vikings' achievements were substantial.

By developing trade routes and craft industries, they revitalised pre-existing urban centres, and they started new towns from Russia to Ireland which are still flourishing today.

They bequeathed to us a vibrant legacy of art and literature and, throughout the far-flung areas in which they settled, they have enriched our languages. In many surprising respects, these notorious people have helped to make us who we are.

1 They Came From the North

Programme outline

Where they came from and where they went

The programme opens with the familiar image of Vikings as raiders, with a dramatic re-enactment of an attack on a monastery. This is immediately followed by scenes which challenge this image. We see a domestic setting and Vikings engaged in trade in the Mediterranean.

We are then introduced to Lucy and Jamie, modern-day children who are visiting their grandad in Shetland, staying in his croft. We are shown the local terrain and then an archaeological dig where we meet Val Turner. The discussion between Val and the children dispels or challenges some of the more popular myths and introduces the potential archaeology has to decipher the Viking way of life.

Val and her colleagues have been excavating an Iron-age site which has thrown up evidence of Viking occupation. They have now moved on to a ruined croft, under which there is evidence for a Viking dwelling. Val, Jamie and Lucy discuss the choice of settlement site, the sorts of conclusions that can be drawn from the findings and the sorts of people who might have lived here.

Next we meet the children's grandad, a storyteller who develops the children's knowledge about the scale and scope of Viking travel, settlement and activity. They learn of the importance of the technology of the longship in enabling the Vikings to travel so far afield, about their religious beliefs and the way they lived. We learn about the Scandinavian landscape and about some of the reasons which might have caused the Vikings to venture so far and to settle in so many different places. We see sites of Viking raids in Ireland, and see them arriving in America and trading in North Africa.

Grandad's story closes with the Norman conquest of England and the fact that many of us throughout the British Isles can trace our ancestry directly to the Scandinavian settlers.

Learning outcomes

Children will:

▶ locate the Viking homelands and the extent of their influence;

▶ ask, and begin to answer, historical questions;

▶ appreciate the role played by archaeology and archaeologists in interpreting the Viking past;

▶ gain insights into aspects of Viking life and society;

▶ begin to appreciate concepts of continuity and change within the Viking context;

▶ develop an understanding of, and empathy with, the Viking perspective.

Key features and vocabulary

Viking, Scandinavia, Norway, Denmark, Sweden, Shetland, archaeology, longship, monastery, jarls/earls, pagan, Christian, lightning raids, settlement, trade, Danelaw, Normandy.

Before viewing

▶ The children could ask family and friends what the word 'Viking' means to them. Do they know anything about the Vikings? A short questionnaire could be used but the questions should be as open-ended as open as possible so that the children receive other people's images (this will enable discussions over issues of historical interpretation).

▶ Ask the children to consider why people might leave the country of their birth nowadays. Make a list together of the reasons offered.

▶ Discuss how people travel today. What types of transport do we have? What technologies are available to us? What are the similarities and differences between then and now?

▶ Draw a large-scale outline map of the Viking world (see the map on page 8 but omit the detail at this stage) and put it up in a prominent place. You can keep referring back to this map as the programmes progress and the children's knowledge develops. They could also have their own outline map.

▶ Set up a simple timeline around the room. Some children may be able to offer dates and events for it as a result of what they have learned from their family and friends. Additions can be made as the programmes are viewed or as chronological information emerges. If no date is offered by the children, tell them that the Vikings were first written about when they raided the monastery on Lindisfarne in AD793 (see Background information on page 4 for this and other events and dates). Write this date on the timeline and add to it as appropriate (make sure there is plenty of room on either side of this date).

▶ Ask the children to listen for any dates that are mentioned in the course of the programme, ready for the timeline.

▶ Hold a brief discussion about what we mean by archaeology. A basic explanation will do at this stage.

Whilst watching

▶ A lot of information is transmitted in the course of the programme, so you may wish to pause the video every so often to confirm understanding or to consolidate it.

▶ You may also decide to take one section of the programme at a time and treat it as a discrete unit. For example, the dig or the sequence showing the grandfather's story-telling would be particularly effective if you choose to focus on the different types of sources relating to a study of the Vikings.

After viewing

▶ This part of the lesson is an opportunity to develop children's literacy skills. For example, you could model note-taking, using the programme and its contents. You may not want to treat the whole programme like this but certainly the last section (when Grandad describes many details about the Viking world) lends itself to a straightforward listing of events and facts. Prioritise together and discuss levels of importance. What have they found interesting, surprising and so on. Why? Explain what you are doing and why. The children could then record their own information in the later programmes.

▶ Display an 'upside-down' map of Scandinavia and northern Europe beside the usual north-south orientation. Discuss how the world might 'look' different from the Scandinavian viewpoint. Would it have been different then? How? Ensure that they identify water as the critical factor in enabling the Vikings to travel so far from home and draw attention to the river systems.

▶ Can the children design a key for the map, now that they have learned about some of the Viking activities overseas? (See the Factfile map for some ideas). They can then begin to enter their own symbols.

▶ Organise them into two groups; one to be Saxon or Celtic inhabitants of Britain or Ireland and the other as inhabitants of Scandinavia. Ask each group to think about how they see the world and the other group.

▶ Review what they have seen in the programme. Why might the Scandinavian group want to come to Britain or Ireland? How would the Saxon, Celtic or British residents feel? Encourage them to think about the range of possibilities in each case. They could present their case to each other or take part in a role play.

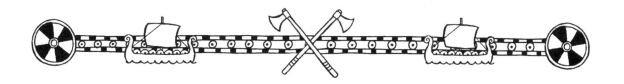

factfile 1

Map of the Viking World

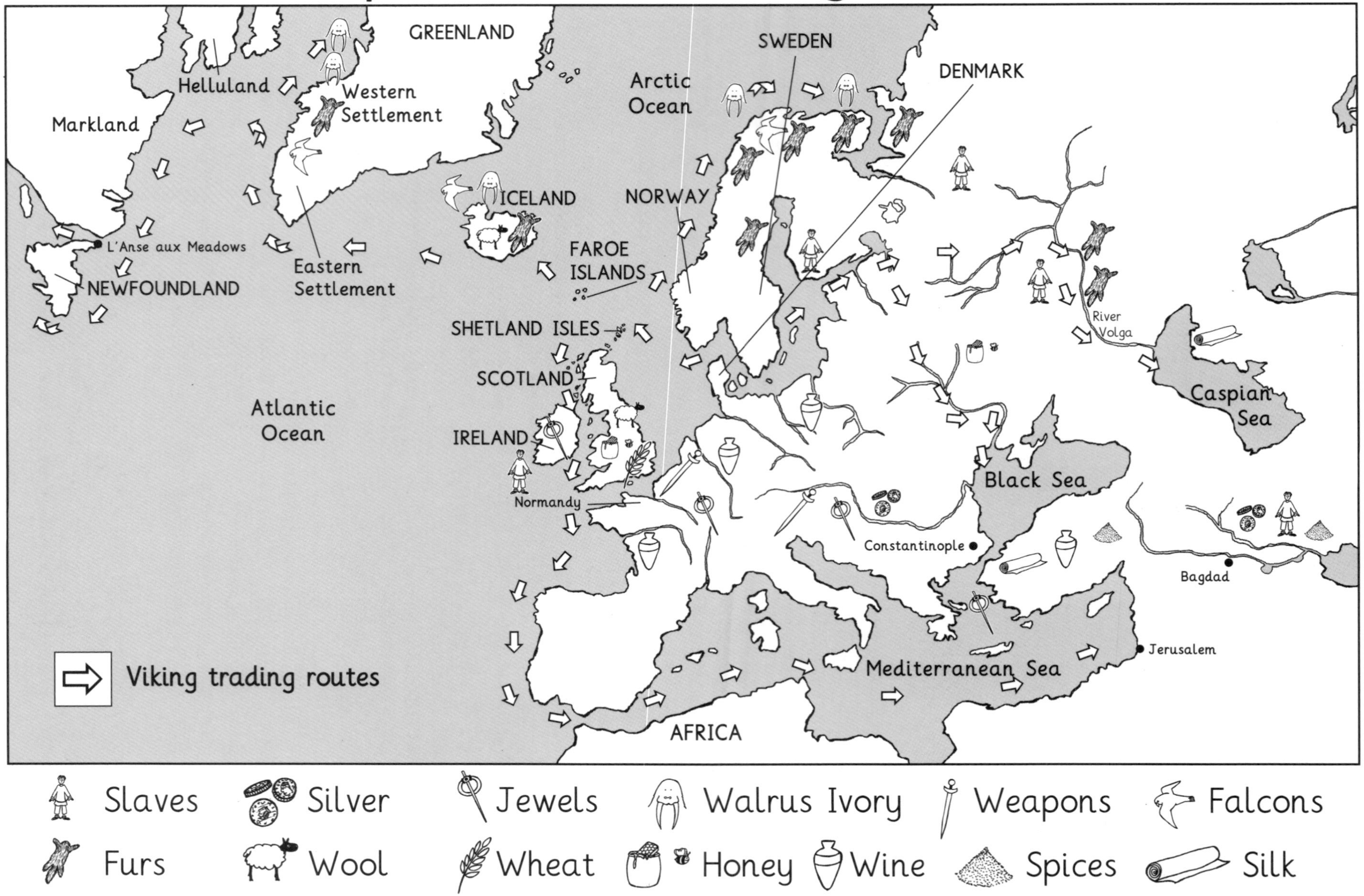
GREENLAND
Helluland
Western Settlement
Markland
ICELAND
NORWAY
SWEDEN
DENMARK
Arctic Ocean
L'Anse aux Meadows
NEWFOUNDLAND
Eastern Settlement
FAROE ISLANDS
SHETLAND ISLES
SCOTLAND
IRELAND
Atlantic Ocean
Normandy
River Volga
Caspian Sea
Black Sea
Constantinople
Bagdad
Jerusalem
Mediterranean Sea
AFRICA
Viking trading routes
Slaves
Furs
Silver
Wool
Jewels
Wheat
Walrus Ivory
Honey
Wine
Weapons
Spices
Falcons
Silk

factfile 2
Viking timeline

around 500-700	The people later known as 'The Vikings' are developing in their Scandinavian homelands (now Norway, Sweden and Denmark).
600-700	Swedish merchants set up trading bases across the Baltic Sea, and begin to explore eastwards along rivers.
700-800	Norwegians begin raiding westwards.
793	Vikings raid the island monastery of Lindisfarne.
795	Vikings raid the monastery on the island of Iona, off the Scottish west coast.
around 800	Vikings from Norway settle in Orkney, Shetland and the Faroe Islands.
828	Vikings invade Ireland.
841	Norwegians develop the town which will become Dublin.
845	Vikings attack Paris.
867	Vikings capture York and by 870 control most of east England, which comes to be known as the Danelaw.
911	Rollo sets up a Viking colony in the west of France, which becomes known as Normandy (North-man's land).
960	King Harald Bluetooth of Denmark becomes Christian. Most Vikings convert to Christianity.
around 982	Eric the Red lands in Greenland.
about 1000	Leif Ericsson reaches America.
1017	King Svein Forkbeard controls England. After he dies, his son Cnut the Great rules England as part of his big empire in Norway, Sweden and Denmark.
1042	King Edward the Confessor retakes England from the Vikings.
1066	King Harald Hardrada of Norway re-invades England, but is killed. The English are then defeated at Hastings by William who came from France, leading the Norman descendants of Rollo's Vikings.
about 1050-1100	The main Viking Age starts to come to an end.
1266	Norway surrenders the Isle of Man and the Hebrides to Scotland.
1468/69	Orkney and Shetland are taken over by Scotland.
about 1450-1500	The last Norse settlements in Greenland die out.

Vikings on the move

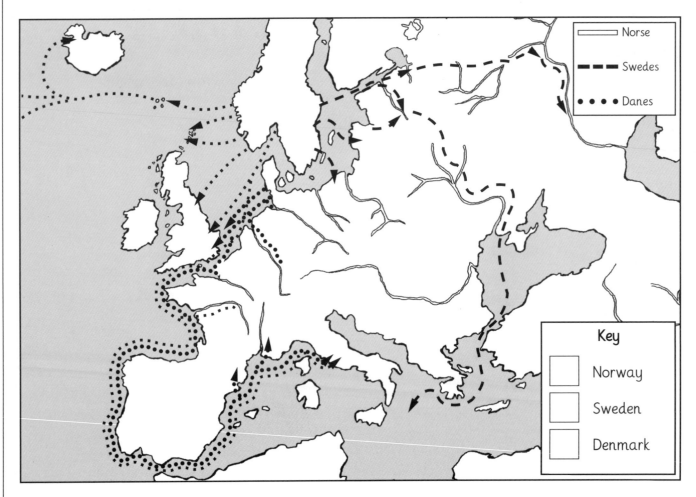

Key: Norse, Swedes, Danes

Key
Norway
Sweden
Denmark

▶ Use an atlas to find Norway, Sweden and Denmark. Write in the names of these three countries on the map above.

▶ Choose a different colour for each of these three countries. Complete the key.

▶ Now colour in the map according to your key. Then colour the lines leading from the countries in the same colour as the country they lead from. These lines show where the Vikings travelled to.

▶ The Vikings are very well known for their ships and were good sailors. Look carefully at the map above. How do you think they were able to travel so far inland? Finish this sentence.

The Vikings were able to reach towns and trading centres far inland

from the coast by using the ....

....

Raids and settlements

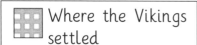 Where the Vikings settled

Shetland Islands

Orkney Isles

Scotland

834

793

Northumbria
Lindisfarne

794
800
844

Strathclyde

Ireland

800

840

Dublin

850

867

York

DANELAW

East Anglia

Wales

855

Mercia

Essex

795
850

836 845

841
834 855

Winchester

851 865

London
Sussex

Cornwall

Wessex

Kent

841

853

838

840

840

841

839

▶ Look at the map above, make a chart like the one below and record the Viking raids on it.

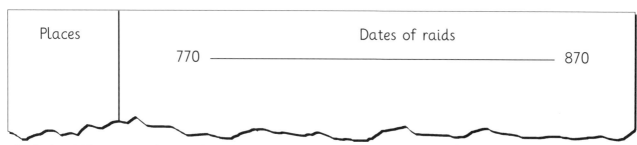

Places	Dates of raids
	770 ——————————————————————— 870

▶ Did the Vikings settle in the places they had raided? If not, why not?

2 The Vikings in Britain

Programme outline

What Viking life was like in this country

Jamie and Lucy follow the progress of the archaeologists at the Viking dig. Val shows them the evidence for a house and helps them to understand what that evidence suggests about its construction. She answers their questions and they discuss various things, such as the ways in which buildings differed across the Viking world, depending on what materials were available locally. They also talk about what it would have been like inside the house and are told about a number of aspects of everyday life. They are shown a replica of a Viking lock and see how the mechanism would have worked.

Over lunch with Grandad, the children hear about Viking ships and we see an example of continuity over time with the construction of boats today on Shetland, using the same techniques as those used by the Vikings.

The discussion then turns to Viking art and crafts and we see examples of fine and intricate silver and metal working, amber jewellery, and carvings. The use of 'runes' is then described before going on to look at sagas as a later method for recording Viking history and literature.

The last part of the programme deals with religion and the role of myth and legend. We learn that the Vikings had their own gods and that only gradually did Christianity become dominant. The value of Viking burials is explained as a way of learning about Viking life, since so many artefacts often accompanied early pagan burials.

The programme closes with Grandad explaining how the Vikings, along with other groups, integrated into early English society and the way that ideas were transmitted.

On the way through the programme, keep an eye and ear out for references to an Arab connection.

Learning outcomes

Children will:

▶ learn about a range of aspects of Viking everyday life;

▶ understand that archaeological evidence can provide valuable insights into those aspects;

▶ appreciate the nature of continuity and change as historical concepts;

▶ gain insight into Viking technology and art techniques.

Key features and vocabulary

archaeology, saga, rune, skald, Valhalla, chess, Christianity, paganism.

Before viewing

▶ Ensure that the children have studied Factfiles 1 and 2, and completed Activity sheets 1 and 2 before watching the next programme. They should be able to locate the different countries in Europe, the Scandinavian countries and those countries which were significant for the Vikings (Ireland, Scotland, Wales, England, Iceland, Greenland, Russia and Newfoundland). Point out the offshore islands of Shetland and Orkney and also the Isle of Man. They should understand the location of the Vikings' origins and eventual settlement. They can now begin to enter some of the detail they have identified on a copy of the large base map taken from the one on page 8.

▶ Ask the children to think about what they could investigate and learn about how the Vikings led their lives. What would they like to know about the Vikings?

▶ Brainstorm what they already know or any ideas they have about the lives Vikings led. Some ideas will come from having seen the programme and others from what they have learned from studying the Anglo-Saxons or Celtic peoples.

▶ Don't worry about misapprehensions at this stage. Record all the ideas on a flipchart or board and, with the children, decide on themes or categories around which to organise their ideas. Some suggestions might be food, buildings, clothes, ships, crafts/skills and gods.

▶ Then ask the children to think up one or more enquiry question for each topic, which they will try to answer from watching the programme and during further research.

▶ Give groups of children responsibility for looking out for information relating to a single topic or question in the programme, with one group having responsibility for noting anything which hadn't been thought of in the brainstorm.

Whilst watching

In addition to focusing on the topic relevant to their group, the children should also concentrate on the programme as a whole. Use your judgement as to whether they should make notes during the programme or whether they make them as a group at the end. They will need time at the end to talk as a group. Model note-taking for them before asking them to do it and/or provide a frame or proforma for them to fill in.

After viewing

▶ Review the programme briefly: What was seen? What wasn't? What was seen that wasn't on the list?

▶ The children should now meet in their groups to pool what they have learned from the programme. What are they investigating? What can they contribute to the collective enquiry about the Vikings in Britain?

▶ The whole class can now begin to build an overview, perhaps adding to the findings through further research. The results could be compiled using a wall display organised around key enquiry questions.

▶ Look at a map of the United Kingdom. Where is your school located? Are you in an area 'occupied' by the Vikings? Using a base map of the UK, the children can shade areas settled by the Vikings and plot their city, town or village.

▶ Choose or make up a short story appropriate to the ages and interests of your class. Tell the story to one group without the others hearing. Send each member of the group to relay the story to another group, pair or individual (ensuring that the story is retold several times, Chinese whispers style). At the feedback stage, make the link with the sagas and how they were constructed. Then ask questions about the sagas as sources of evidence for the Vikings.

▶ Look carefully with the children at a range of motifs and designs found on Viking jewellery and wooden and stone carvings. Ask them to design either a cover page or a title panel for the wall display, incorporating some of the design ideas they have encountered.

factfile 3
Viking houses

The different kinds of houses that the Vikings built were a result of where they lived. Farms and fishing settlements were set in landscapes where climates and local building materials differed. In forested lands, log cabins or wooden plank walls were common. In treeless areas, walls were often made from turf blocks on stone foundations, with roof frames made from driftwood or even whale ribs. Sometimes, timber house kits were imported. One house, in the treeless Faroe Islands, may be the oldest European timber building still lived in today. Roofs were made from turf, thatch or wooden shingles. Room dividers (and sometimes outside walls) might be made from 'wattle and daub' – sticks which were woven and then draftproofed by daubing on clay or manure.

Indoors, the homes differed according to the size and importance of the family. Fashions changed through time. Sagas and archaeological evidence show that one type of home had a long living room, with wide benches on both sides where people could sit and work or chat during the day, then at night sleep in rows with their feet towards a long central fire hearth.

factfile 4

Laws and 'Things'

People think of the Vikings as lawless, and they certainly could be cruel and without mercy. But amongst themselves they had great respect for laws, particularly if these were agreed by communities at public meetings where free men and women could speak.

The Vikings' name for a public meeting was a 'Thing'. Place names such as Tingwall in Shetland show where they once met. Even today the Tynwald of the Isle of Man, which is part of Britain, is still governed in this way, which was inherited from the Vikings.

There were small 'Things' for local matters, and some for bigger regions. From about AD902, Iceland held an 'Althing' for the whole country (one of the earliest democratic national parliaments ever) at a place called Thingvellir. People travelled very long distances to camp there at midsummer. They never built a town there, not wanting their Althing to become dominated by permanent politicians.

Since most people could not read, each year a Lawspeaker recited part of the Lawcode. This Lawcode was named 'Grey Goose'. People are still suggesting reasons for this name.

Fines for injuring somebody included paying the doctor's bills. For manslaughter, payment must be made to the victim's family. There were no prisons, so people were often banished from their own country. This might be for a number of years. For a really nasty murder, anyone who caught the outlaw could legally put him to death.

Some laws were for control of the violent or powerful, but other laws ensured that the community cared for the weak or vulnerable, including orphan children. It was a duty to plough old people's fields before your own.

Women had important rights. Slavery of captured women and men (thralls) was common, and they might be treated harshly or even killed. However, Viking laws were strong on the rights of their own women, whose importance was recognised more than that of many other women elsewhere. With men often away raiding, trading, fishing and hunting, women managed farms, craft industries and commerce, as well as bringing up families wisely. From the age of 15, a girl could choose her own husband, though the richer they were, the more likely their marriage would be arranged to link powerful families. It was accepted that husbands might have children by slaves, while wives were meant to be faithful. But if a husband was uncaring or beat his wife, she had the right to divorce him, just by making a statement in front of witnesses. Sagas show respect for women's cleverness and bravery, while rich burials, such as the Oseberg ship, show clearly how highly they were thought of.

Overall, the Icelandic Vikings had better civil rights laws than in many parts of the world today.

Leaving home

▶ Use this spidergram to record your notes and thoughts about the Vikings leaving home and settling in other places.

Reasons for leaving Scandinavia

....

....

....

....

Places they went to

....

....

....

....

Clues for archaeologists (what they left behind)

....

....

....

....

Leaving home

What they needed to settle

....

....

....

....

Reasons why they might have left home

....

....

....

....

What might their survival kit have been?

....

....

....

....

Viking homes

▶ Look at this plan of a real Viking home. The ruins were found in Iceland. The house was destroyed by a volcano about 1000 years ago.

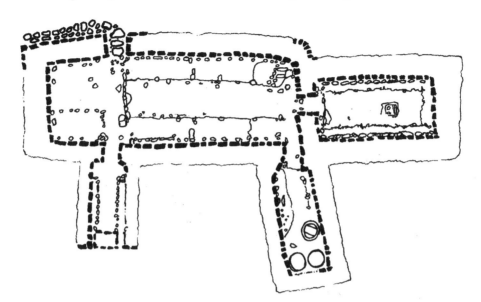

▶ This is a drawing of how the house would have looked. The outside is covered in turf. Write some sentences to describe what it would have been like to live in this house. Think about the weather, the light and the smells. Use reference books to find out about the furniture the Vikings might have used.

....

....

....

....

....

....

3 Digging up the Vikings

Programme outline

The evidence

The children return to the dig and discover that significant progress has been made in uncovering the longhouse. Val helps them to interpret what they can see. We learn some of the basic techniques of archaeology from Val's explanation of soil layers and analyses of objects associated with a site, and the sorts of clues certain objects give us, such as coins and amber beads. She also emphasises the importance of recording accurately the finds that are made.

That evening, the children share a barbecue with their grandfather, which is an attempt to imitate a Viking feast. Grandad explains the value of using replicas of objects, such as cooking utensils. Then, by looking at boats like the Viking longship they begin to understand something of the Vikings' achievements. Through the programme we learn about the continuing tradition in Shetland of boatbuilding, using the same techniques that the Vikings used. Grandad then draws the children's attention to the legacy passed to us via the Vikings but from further afield. For example, from Mediterranean trading links came chess and a special type of mill which they imported into their settled lands.

The last section of the programme investigates the extent of the Viking legacy in our everyday lives, such as place names, derived language, Viking sites and buildings, sagas which feature heroes and the gods, contemporary festivals and celebrations which are directly linked to earlier Viking ones.

The programme closes with a Viking scene which looks like the site excavated by the archaeologists, but is now peopled with Viking children resembling Lucy and Jamie, who are engaged in crofting a thousand years ago.

Learning outcomes

Children will:

▶ gain deeper understanding of the ways in which archaeological evidence can help to interpret the past;

▶ appreciate the contribution made by other disciplines, such as forensic science, in helping to understand the past;

▶ feel a sense of wonder at coming into close contact with the people of the past through their dwellings and artefacts;

▶ understand something of the possibilities and the limitations of reconstructing the past;

▶ extend their knowledge and understanding of some of the Vikings' technologies;

▶ appreciate the ways that ideas, inventions and pastimes were transmitted from one culture to another;

▶ develop an understanding of the Viking legacy and the physical evidence we have around us.

Key features and vocabulary

Longhouse, finds, soil layer, replica, Shetland yole (small boat), click mill, chess, berserker, gods, Thor's day etc, place names, language, heritage, legacy.

Before viewing

▶ Set up a dig, either in the classroom or in the school grounds. Collect a mixture of small, large, delicate and clumsy objects made from a range of materials. Include tools, coins, jewellery and pottery. Place the objects in layers with the oldest ones at the bottom.

▶ Use this to discuss with the children how a dig works. Why are the layers important? What objects might survive best? Why? What sorts of things might we leave behind and what will people living after us make of our civilisation?

▶ Talk about making reconstructions and trying to reconstruct things that happened in the past. These are difficult ideas which will benefit from being talked through. What are the difficulties? What is the value for historians and archaeologists?

Whilst watching

▶ Ask the children to look out for and list examples of historical reconstruction.

After viewing

▶ Rewind the tape to the part where the archaeologists have found the mystery object (counter number?). Pause the video and ask the children to hypothesise: What is it? What was it for? Can they extend the drawing?

▶ Review the list of reconstructions the children have identified. Discuss with them what evidence there is likely to be for each one. What questions do they want to ask of the children and their grandfather?

▶ Provide a range of craft materials and ask the children to make copies of Viking objects. Make sure that they review what they have done and evaluate the 'history' involved. They could make a museum collection and the objects' labels could describe how they differ from the originals. Alternatively, this could be done in an extended piece of writing using a writing frame.

▶ Have another look at the developing class map together. Add any further information from this programme. Can you find a way of recording the Viking contacts which brought chess and the click mill to Europe?

▶ Read together an example of Viking literature, either a saga or some poems. You could use the text of the saga on Page 23 (Njal's saga). Discuss it afterwards. Who are the characters? What do they do in the story?

(In addition to the suggested questions on the sheet, there is considerable scope here for literacy-related activities. The children can read the passage for language of movement, for epic qualities and also for story structure. They could reduce the story to half a dozen main points or sentences. Finally, one child or the teacher could assume the role of storyteller; what actions will s/he use to dramatise the story and what sounds could s/he make?)

▶ The children should have acquired a significant amount of knowledge and understanding about the Vikings and their way of life and will be in a good position to undertake an empathetic activity. Taking the Viking longhouse of the Shetland dig as a focus (or another of your choice), revise with them the kind of things a dig can tell archaeologists about the building and the activity inside it. Add information as necessary or appropriate (see Factfile 5). Help them to record their information. Now, can they place themselves inside the longhouse during a winter's evening. What is it like? Who is there? What are they doing? What are the sounds, the smells, the sights?

▶ Ask the children to reconstruct the scene in writing. Alternative methods of recording could be a role play, a cartoon strip or a taped or oral presentation.

factfile 5
Viking burials

We know more about the earlier Vikings than the later ones. This is because from about AD950, more and more Vikings became Christians and so were not buried in the Viking way, which was with lots of different objects which they believed would be useful after death.

Archaeologists find a lot of evidence from the burials about the Viking people and what they did. Some people were buried in a boat or ship, such as the Oseberg ship which was a burial place for some important Viking women. Rich people were buried with jewellery, warriors with their weapons, and craftworkers with the tools of their trades. Merchants were buried with scales to weigh silver, and coins and gifts, which often tell about trade routes. Unfortunately, much of the evidence we need to understand the past often rots or rusts away in the ground. Cloth almost never survives, and wood usually leaves only faint traces.

Viking sagas were not written down until a long time after the stories were first told. Evidence from archaeology shows that some of what the writers of sagas imagined about earlier times was not always right. According to Viking sagas, the shoes of dead people were sometimes tied on the wrong feet, so the dead Viking couldn't trot back to haunt you! However, since boots rot away, we don't have the evidence to prove that!

As buried

As excavated

factfile 6
Viking ships and boats

Today, 1000 years after the Viking Age, some boats are still being built in the Viking way, both in Scandinavia and where Vikings settled, such as Shetland and Fair Isle. These modern boats are like some small Viking ones, which were found buried with a longship in Norway, because their design is the very best for rowing and sailing in northern seas.

To make these boats, the Vikings used thin, springy boards, overlapping them so their edges could be fixed together with nails bent over washers. This is called 'clinker building'. In other kinds of boats, a stiff skeleton with heavy ribs is made before adding planks of wood. The Viking way is to shape the hull from the thin boards, then afterwards add just enough ribs for strengthening. This makes the hull very light, but very strong because of its springiness (like a light fishing rod, which would snap if it was stiff).

Lightness made it possible to haul the boats overland between seaways or between rivers, which is how the Vikings crossed Europe. Lightness and springiness together help fast rowing and sailing through pounding waves. The edges of the overlapping boards also create froth so that clinker-built boats skim along faster than boats which sit deep in the water. Viking ships could sail from Norway to Iceland in seven days, and Iceland to Ireland in four days.

People did not believe the saga stories about giant Dragon Ships until 1997 when a 35-metre longship was discovered in Denmark.

War ship's figure head

Clinker building

Digging up one Viking

▶ Look carefully at this diagram of a Viking grave and the objects found there. Match the numbered objects in the grave with the key. Write the numbers by the names of the objects.

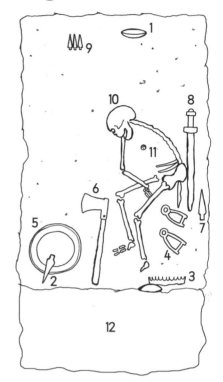

Key

____ spearheads   ____ arrowheads

____ comb   ____ the body

____ stirrups   ____ Arabic coin

____ bowl   ____ round metal

____ axe   'bosses' (centres)

____ knife   of shields

____ sword

▶ Now look carefully at this picture. Put the same numbers by the objects in the picture.

▶ Something is missing by the number 12 in the diagram. Can you guess what it is? (Look very carefully at the drawing.)

....

▶ Why have some things survived 1000 years in the grave?

....

....

....

....

▶ Why have some things rotted away?

....

....

....

....

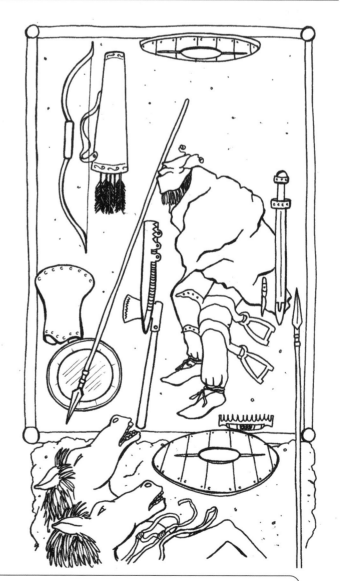

Njal's story – A Viking saga

One morning a Viking called Njal met his friend Skarphedin who had a small round shield and an axe. With him was Kari in a silken jacket and gilded helmet, with a shield that had painted on it the figure of a lion. There was also Helgi wearing a blue tunic of dyed cloth with a silver belt, blue striped trousers and black boots. On his head was an iron helmet and he carried a long sword and a spear with a broad blade and thick shaft.

Njal wore a heavy shirt of metal rings and a thick cloak made of skins. As they went hunting an enemy called Thrain, they met Gunnar. Gunnar was tall and strong and well skilled in the use of arms. He could use the sword well and deal blows so swiftly that three swords seemed to flash through the air at the same time. He had no equal in shooting with a bow. In full armour he could leap higher than his own height and jump as far backwards as forwards.

He joined Njal because Thrain had killed his brother. After days of searching they found the evil Thrain but he was on the other side of an icy river and had ten men with him. Njal and his men charged down to the river's edge. Thrain and his men stood on an icy patch near an ice flow. Skarphedin, with axe raised, ran down to the river. It was so deep there was no place to wade across. Skarphedin took a running start and leapt forward on to the ice flow with the speed of a bird. Thrain was just about to put on his helmet as Skarphedin bore down on him and struck him with his axe 'Battle Troll'. The axe split Thrain's head right down so that his teeth dropped on to the ice.

▶ Read Njal's saga. Remember that this saga was written down several lifetimes after the event is meant to have taken place.

▶ Using three different colours, mark the story to show:
1) The clothes warriors wore 3) Brave deeds and heroic acts
2) The weapons they used

▶ Why do you think the description of the clothes and weapons are so detailed?

....

....

▶ What will you remember most from the story?

....

....

Further information

Further Reading

Batey, C., Clark, H., Page, R., and Price, N. – *Cultural Atlas of the Viking World*, Andromeda Oxford 1994 – ISBN 0 8160 30049

Else Roesdahl – *The Vikings (Revised Edition)*, Penguin Books 1998 2nd edition paperback – ISBN 0 14 025282 7

John Haywood – *The Penguin Historical Atlas of the Vikings*, Penguin Books 1995 paperback – ISBN 0 14 0 51328 0

Peter Sawyer (ed) – *The Oxford Illustrated History of the Vikings*, Oxford UP 1997 – ISBN 0 19 820526 0

Editors of Time-Life Books: *Lost Civilisations Series: Vikings – Raiders from the North*, Time-Life 1994 – ISBN 0 8094 9895 2

John Clare – *I Was There: Vikings, Riverswift* (Random House) 1994 – ISBN 1 898304 629

Judith Jesch – *Women in the Viking Age*, Boydell Press 1991 – ISBN 0 85115 278 3

Britta Nurmann et al – *The Vikings Recreated in Colour Photographs*, Europa Militaria Special No6, Windrow and Greene 1997 – ISBN 1 85915 058 6

Anne Civardi and James Graham-Campbell – *Viking Raiders (new edition)*, Usborne 1997 paperback – ISBN 0 74603073 8

David Wilson – *The Vikings Activity Book*, British Museum Publications paperback, frequently reprinted – ISBN 0 7141 0549 X

Places to visit

The Jorvik Centre at York is the major UK presentation geared up for children.

Jarlshof in Shetland is less accessible, but very relevant to the Shetland focus of our films. The interpretative booklet is excellent: succinct and inexpensive but authoritative and well illustrated. Published by Historic Scotland 1993, Jarlshof – *A Walk Through the Past* – ISBN 0 7480 0460 2.